{ Cape Penguin }

{ Common Frog }

# *Bone Collection*
# ANIMALS

{ Green Turtle }

{ Platypus }

Copyright © 2013 by Marshall Editions

Published by A & C Black, an imprint of Bloomsbury Publishing Plc
50 Bedford Square, London, WC1B 3DP

www.bloomsbury.com

ISBN 978-1-4729-0401-0

A CIP record for this book is available from the British Library.

Produced for Marshall Editions by Tall Tree Ltd
Written by: Rob Colson
Illustrated by: Sandra Doyle, Elizabeth Gray and Steve Kirk
Designed by: Marisa Renzullo
Consultant: Camilla de la Bédoyère


Printed and bound in China


1 3 5 7 9 10 8 6 4 2

## PICTURE CREDITS

Alamy: 35 vario images, 47mr imagebroker; Corbis: 34-35 Roy Toft; Creative Commons: 38b Nachoman-au, 79b Christian Mehlführer; Dreamstime: 23br Tjkphotography, 89 Raycan, 90tr Marek Uliasz; FLPA: 4H, 50br Robin Chittenden, 4tr, 31tr, 31b Photo Researchers, 8, 16, 18r, 68, 79mr Imagebroker, 9 Jan Van Arkel, 101, 10-11, 63b R Dirscherl, 11H Mike Parr, 11tr, 181, 30-31, 59nr, 87mr Konrad Wothe, 11mr Norbert Probst, 13 Rene Krekels, 14t, 15mr Emanuele Biggi, 14b, 24, 76, 77, 83mr M&P Fogden, 15ml, 25, 26-27, 67tr, 83H Pete Oxford, 17, 28, 59br, 60, 61, 62ml Hiroya Minakuchi, 19H Chien Lee, 19tr, 37, 58tr, 74l, 87b Mitsuaki Iwago, 19mr Michel Gunther, 20 Fritz Polking, 21 WG Algöwer, 22l Christian Heinrich, 22m, 84 Ingo Arndt, 22r Chris Mattison, 23ml, 29, 67bl, 81, 83tr ZSSD, 28 Hiroya, 30l Tom Vezo, 32, 62-63, 63m Biosphoto, 33, 39mr, 40, 87t Gerard Lacz, 34 ml Terry Whittaker, 34bl, 66-67, 70r Tui De Roy, 64, 79ml, 80, 86r Frans Lanting, 39b Shin Yoshiro, 41 Theo Allofs, 42t Martin Willis, 42-43, 73 J&C Sohns, 48 Momatiuk&Eastcott, 50l Mike Lane, 5lm Michael Durham, 51b Dietmar Nill, 52 Suzi Eszterhas, 53, 65, 71m, 71b Richard Du Toit, 54-55 Tim Fitzharris, 54t Bernd Rohrschneider, 55bl Thomas Marent, 56, 57 John Eastcott, 58l Gerry Ellis, 59t Sergey Gorshkov, 62t, 75br, 90l C&T Stuart, 63t Theo Allofs, 66l David Hosking, 67H Egmont Strigl, 69, 70bl Michio Hoshino, 71tr Ignacio Yufera, 78l David Tipling, 78r Thomas Marent, 79t Albert Visage, 82l, 82r Luciano Candisani, 86l Cyril Ruoso, 90br, 91tr Flip Nicklin, 91H Mike Parry; Getty: 39H, 39tr Dea Picture Library; Istockphoto: 90m Denis Kozlenko; NHPA: 26l Martin Wendler, 27H Larry Ditto, 27tr, 27mr Stephen Dalton; Shutterstock: 23H anekoho, 23tr Denton Rumsey, 30m jps, 35mr Gilad Rom, 38t John Carnemolla, 43t worldswildlifewonders, 43b PA Jacks, 44 ecoprint, 45 gallimaufry, 46tr ana23885475, 46m, 47tr Ivan Kuzmin, 46b Hugh Lansdown, 47H Eric Isselee, 47b Morphart Creation, 54mr taviphoto, 54b Johan Barnard, 55br Stuart Taylor, 62bl Ignacio Salaverria, 66bl Hein Nouwens, 66br Rich Koele, 67br Mari Swanepoel, 70ml Sergey Uryadnikov, 71H Colette3, 72 ale rizzo, 74bl Daniel Gale, 74-75 Olga l, 75t Robert Adrian Hillman, 75mr Four Oaks, 85 Hill2k, 88 bikeriderlondon, 91m mart, 91bl skyhawk, 91br antoniomas; SPL: 31H GS Grant, 47mr, 91mr Bo Veisland

# Bone Collection
# ANIMALS

A & C BLACK
AN IMPRINT OF BLOOMSBURY

# CONTENTS

# INTRODUCTION

OUR bony skeletons support and protect our bodies. Without our bones, we would collapse into jelly on the floor! Our skeletons have joints and are attached to muscles, and this allows us to move around. Lots of other animals have skeletons like ours. In this book, we get under the skin of some of them.

{ Fig 1: Indian palm squirrel }

{ Fig 2: Toucan }

We will show you a drawing of the skeleton of one species of animal. These drawings are based on real skeletons, and you'll see exactly how the bones fit together. We then take a closer look at similar animals, showing you how they live and explaining how different parts of their bodies work. Finally, we will look at the human skeleton, and you will see just how much we have in common with the animals around us!

{ Fig 3: Pit viper skeleton }

# ANIMALS WITH BACKBONES

THE animals featured in this book are all vertebrates. This means that they have a skeleton with a backbone. Vertebrates come in many different shapes and sizes, but under the skin, they have surprisingly similar skeletons. The backbone extends from the head, where the brain is protected by a skull. Nerves run along the backbone carrying signals between the brain and the body. Compare the skeletons to one another, and you will see that the bodies of many animals have the same parts, with rib cages to protect important organs such as the heart and lungs, and with arms, legs, flippers or wings extending from the central body.

Shoulder

Elbow

Radius and ulna

### Early mammals

Bats, seals and humans belong to a group of animals called placental mammals. All the placental mammals alive today have evolved from a common ancestor that looked like a shrew and lived around 80 million years ago, when dinosaurs still walked the Earth.

# FIRST VERTEBRATE

Scientists think that all vertebrate animals evolved from a small fish-like creature that lived more than 500 million years ago. It was similar to the lamprey, which is still found in rivers and oceans today. Like the lamprey, the first vertebrates did not have jaws. Instead, they had funnel-like mouths, which they used to suck food into their stomachs.

{ Fig I: Sea lamprey }

## COMPARING BONES

Here, we've put the bones of the wing of a fruit bat, the flipper of an elephant seal and the arm of a human next to each other. Can you tell which is which? The bat's wing is used to fly, the seal's flipper to swim and a human's arm to pick things up. They all look very different from the outside, but the bones underneath the skin are arranged in the same way. All three have shoulder blades, upper arm and lower arm bones, and "hands" with five "fingers".

"Finger" bones

Shoulder

Shoulder

Humerus

"Hand" bones

# ATLANTIC COD

A LARGE fish that lives in the North Atlantic Ocean, the Atlantic cod is a powerful predator. It has a sensitive whisker, called a barbel, on its chin, which it uses to find prey on the seabed.

## DORSAL FINS
Each fin contains lots of small bones called fin rays.

Eye socket

Pectoral fins

## FIERCE HUNTER
Cod hunt shrimps, crabs and small fish such as herring.

Pelvic fins

## FIN CONTROL

The fish pushes itself forwards with its dorsal, anal and tail fins. It uses its pectoral and pelvic fins to change direction.

### Fishing industry

Every year, nearly a million tonnes of cod are caught by fishermen. Their numbers have fallen sharply, and this has led to calls for a reduction in fishing.

Tail fin

Vertebrae

Anal fins

A fully grown Atlantic cod weighs up to 25 kg and is more than 1 m long.

## COLD WATERS

Atlantic cod live in cold, shallow water around the coasts of North America and northern Europe. They swim together in large shoals, and feed at mid-depths or near the sea floor.

# FISH

FISH have been around for 500 million years. They were the earliest animals to have backbones. Fish breathe with gills, which take oxygen from the water.

Sailfish

## LARVAE

Fish lay large numbers of small eggs. The eggs hatch into young called larvae. Many fish feed on larvae and most will be eaten, but some survive and grow into adults.

### BOTTOM FEEDER
The plaice lies on its side, hiding on the seabed. Both of its eyes are on the same side of its head, so it can still see.

## FASTEST FISH
The sailfish is the fastest fish. It can swim at a speed of 110 km/h.

Long pectoral fin ➤

### SAIL FIN
When it feels threatened, the sailfish raises up its sail-like dorsal fin to make itself look big and scary.

## Bendy body

The skeletons of sharks are not made of bone. Instead, they are made of bendy cartilage – the material your nose is made from. This makes them very flexible.

{ Fig 1: Gill slits }

Sharks have 5-7 gill slits on each side of the head.

Spear-like bill

Skin changes colour when the fish is excited.

## SAFETY IN NUMBERS

Many smaller fish swim in large shoals. This makes it harder for predators to catch them.

## DEEP-SEA MONSTER

The viperfish spends its days in the deep oceans where it is totally dark. The fish makes its own light from special organs on the side of its body. Other fish are attracted to the light, and the viperfish snatches them in its large jaws when they draw near.

{ Fig 2: Sloane's viperfish }

# COMMON FROG

Large skull

THE common frog is an amphibian, which means that it can live on land and in water. It has lungs to breathe air, but it can also take in oxygen through its skin, which allows it to survive long periods underwater.

### INSECT HUNTER
The common frog hunts insects, spiders, slugs and snails. It catches its prey with its long, sticky tongue.

Front feet

The front legs are much smaller than the back legs.

## BACKBONE

Frogs have very short spines. This keeps their backs rigid when they jump.

## HIP BONES

The frog uses its long hip bones to power its leaps.

This frog is about 10 cm long. It is small enough to sit on the palm of your hand.

Thigh bone

## WINTER SLEEP

The common frog spends most of its time on land, hunting in woodlands and fields. But it never strays far from water. Every winter, it finds a damp place under a stone or in a shallow pond, where it hibernates.

The long back feet have webbed toes, which help the frog to swim.

# AMPHIBIANS

FROGS, newts and salamanders are amphibians. Most amphibians spend some time out of the water, but they must keep their skin moist, as this helps them breathe.

## CROAKING FROGS

Male frogs croak, or call, to attract females. The females prefer males with loud, deep calls. The males make their calls louder and deeper by inflating special vocal sacs under their mouths.

## NEWTS

Newts have lizard-shaped bodies, with short legs. They swim using their long, flattened tails.

Vocal sac

Dainty tree frog

14

# TADPOLES

When they hatch, frog larvae are known as tadpoles. They feed and grow in the water, and within a few weeks, they turn into tiny froglets. The froglets grow into full-size adults over the next one or two years.

*{ Fig 2: Froglet }*

*{ Fig 1: Tadpole }*

## Caecilian

This creature looks like a giant worm, but it is actually a type of amphibian. Caecilians live underground. They burrow through the soil in search of insects and worms to eat.

## GIANT SALAMANDER

This is the biggest amphibian of all, growing up to 1.8 m long. It feeds on frogs, fish and mice.

## AXOLOTL

The axolotl spends all its life in water. It breathes through its feather-like gills.

## WATER TO LAND

Most amphibians lay their eggs in water. The eggs hatch into larvae, which look very different from the adults. The larvae stay in the water until they have developed into miniature versions of their parents.

# GREEN TURTLE

**GREEN** sea turtles are large reptiles that live in warm tropical oceans. They cruise across the oceans, grazing on lush meadows of sea grass and seaweed.

The bones at the top of the head are fused together to form a protective helmet.

## BONY SHELL

The turtle's skeleton is surrounded by a hard shell. The rib cage and backbone are joined to a layer of bone. This layer is covered by plates, or scutes, made from keratin – the hard substance that your fingernails are made from.

### Ocean wanderer

The green sea turtle pulls itself through the water using its long front flippers. The flippers work like oars, beating in the shape of a figure of eight.

Shoulder and hip bones are inside the ribcage.

The paddle-like flippers contain bones similar to our hands, with five sets of "finger" bones.

## HARD BEAK
Green sea turtles have horny beaks with saw-like edges, which they use to scrape algae off hard surfaces.

Back flippers are used for steering.

Green sea turtles grow up to 1.5 m long, and can weigh 150 kg – the weight of two adult humans.

Fused ribs

# TURTLES

WHEN turtles sense danger, they pull their heads and legs inside their shells. Turtles live on land and in water and have flippers. Turtles that live only on land are called tortoises. Tortoises have a more domed shell and feet with small claws instead of flippers.

## LONG LIVES

Turtles can live for a very long time. Giant tortoises have been known to live for more than 200 years!

Giant tortoise

Mouth has a hard beak but no teeth.

## HATCHLINGS

The first year of a turtle's life is a very dangerous time. Only 1 per cent of these hatchlings will make it to adulthood.

Tortoises have legs and feet rather than flippers.

{ Fig 1: Green turtle hatchling }

When they hatch, the young turtles pull themselves out of the sand and make their way to the sea.

## Laying eggs

Like most reptiles, turtles lay eggs. Sea turtles lay their eggs on beaches, where they bury the eggs in the sand to keep them safe.

## HINGED SHELL

A turtle's shell covers all of its body except the head and legs. The top side is called the carapace, while the bottom side is called the plastron. In some turtles, the plastron is hinged. This allows the animal to pull its head and legs inside the shell for extra safety.

### TAKING REFUGE

This young spotted pond turtle has pulled itself right inside its shell.

## BREATHING UNDERWATER

Turtles breathe air using lungs, just like us. But some turtles also breathe underwater, like fish. The pig-nosed turtle takes water in through its mouth and passes it out through its large nostrils. A special lining in the mouth absorbs oxygen from the water.

{ Fig 2: Pig-nosed turtle }

19

# NILE CROCODILE

THIS fearsome reptile has been ambushing unsuspecting victims ever since the time of the dinosaurs. The Nile crocodile is at home on land or in the water, and few animals are safe from its attacks.

Strong, flexible backbone

Teeth are replaced when they wear out.

Long jaws are studded with sharp teeth.

## KEEP BACK!

You might outsprint a Nile crocodile on land, but in water it can move ten times faster than you. It hides in the water and ambushes large mammals such as antelopes, which come to the waterside to drink.

# HIGH WALK

On land, the crocodile moves around mostly by sliding on its belly. But it can run in short bursts by raising itself off the ground in a "high walk" as the skeleton here is doing.

## Growing menace

Crocodiles live for up to 100 years, and they keep growing all their lives. As they grow, their prey changes. The young hunt fish and frogs, while larger adults take on wildebeest and zebras.

## MUSCULAR TAIL

Crocodiles swim by swinging their strong, flat tails from side to side.

Legs raise the body off the ground when running.

## WEBBED FEET

The four toes on the back foot are webbed. This helps the crocodile to steer as it swims.

A mature male Nile crocodile can measure more than 5 m long and weigh up to 1 tonne.

# CROCODILIANS

THE crocodilians are a group of reptiles that includes crocodiles, alligators and gharials. They are strong swimmers and spend much of their lives in water.

Mouth contains 24 sharp teeth.

## POWERFUL BITE

The muscles that close a crocodile's jaws are very powerful. But the muscles that open the mouth are weak – so weak that a human can hold a large crocodile's mouth shut.

{ Fig 1: Scales }

The skin is protected by a layer of tough, horny scales.

## ALLIGATOR

With a wider snout than a crocodile's, an alligator's teeth fit inside its mouth when it's closed.

## Keeping cool

When they fall asleep in the hot sun, crocodiles are in danger of overheating. They stay cool by sleeping with their mouths wide open.

## HIDDEN DANGER

The nose and eyes of an alligator are at the top of its head. This allows it to float almost entirely underwater, hiding from its prey.

## GHARIAL

The long-snouted gharial lives in rivers and swamps in southern Asia.

## FISH-EATER

The gharial spends almost all its time in the water, feeding on a diet of fish. It swishes its narrow snout swiftly through the water to catch its fast-moving prey. It then holds on to the slippery meal with its many needle-like teeth.

## CARING MOTHER

Just before they hatch, baby crocodiles cry out to their mother from inside their eggs. This makes sure that the mother is there to guard them when they emerge. The mother carefully carries the hatchlings to the safety of the water in her mouth.

{ Fig 2: Crocodile mother }

23

# PIT VIPER

**PITS**
The small heat-sensitive pits are found just above the front of the upper jaw.

**FANGS**
Venom is pumped into the fangs from glands on either side of the head. The venom is injected when the fangs pierce the prey's skin.

THIS pit viper lives in the forests of America. It hunts in the dark with amazing accuracy. On each side of its head is a small pit that is sensitive to heat. When an animal comes near, the snake senses its body heat with these pits and knows just where to strike!

Back bone

### Open wide

The viper's lightweight skull is made mostly of jaw bones. It can open its mouth very wide because its upper and lower jaws are loosely joined. This allows the snake to swallow large prey whole.

24

# NIGHT SENSES

The two heat-sensitive pits, one on either side of the head, produce a stereo effect, allowing the snake to judge distance as well as direction. This means that the snake can strike with perfect accuracy, even in pitch darkness.

Ribs

The viper grows up to 3 m in length – that's longer than an adult human!

Most snakes do not have hip bones, shoulder blades or leg bones.

The pit viper's skeleton is mostly made up of vertebrae, each with a pair of ribs attached. This snake has about 200 pairs of ribs.

# SNAKES

WHEN hunting, snakes use many ways to kill prey and to see off any predators.

## CRAWLING HUNTER

Slithering about on its stomach, a snake can detect the tiniest vibrations in the ground. These could be made by a scuttling mouse, or they could be made by a mongoose that wants to eat the snake!

## CRUSHED TO DEATH

Constrictors coil their powerful bodies around prey and then squeeze the life out of them!

## UNDER THREAT

When a predator comes near, a rattlesnake rears up and shakes its rattle as a warning.

Scales

## Warning signs

Some of the most venomous snakes are also the most brightly coloured. This coral snake has bright bands of orange and yellow to warn any would-be hunters that it has a deadly bite.

{ Fig 1: Fang }

The hollow fangs pierce the skin and inject the venom.

Eyes

Tongue

## SNAKE SENSES

When a snake flicks out its forked tongue, it is actually smelling the air. The tongue collects scent molecules and then passes these to a sensor, called the Jacobson's organ, in the roof of the mouth.

### SHARP STRIKE

When a viper bites, it opens its mouth wide and the long fangs flick forwards before they are injected into its prey.

## SEA SNAKE

Found in the warm waters of the Indian and Pacific oceans, sea snakes are some of the most venomous snakes on the planet. They spend most of their lives in the water, but still need to surface to breathe.

{ Fig 2: Banded sea snake }

# SCARLET MACAW

Birds do not have teeth. They use their beaks to break up their food.

Backbone

THE scarlet macaw is a parrot that lives in the lush rainforests of South America. It feeds on nuts and seeds, which it crushes with its large beak. Parrots are very intelligent birds that are great at solving puzzles. They use twigs and leaves as tools to crack open nuts.

Breastbone

## STANDING FIRM

Each foot has four toes. Two toes point forwards and two point backwards. This allows the bird to grip on to branches.

# COLOUR VISION

Birds can see a colour called ultraviolet that we can't see. Scarlet macaws look spectacular to us with their red and blue feathers, but they probably look even more colourful to each other!

## Keeping in touch

Macaws fly together in pairs but sometimes come together in larger family groups. They keep in contact with others in their group by making loud screeching calls that can be heard several kilometres away.

Humerus

The scarlet macaw measures 80 cm from its head to the tips of its tail feathers.

Tail bone

Short finger bones have tiny wings, called alulas, attached to them.

A bird's wing has arm and finger bones. The main flight feathers, called primaries, are attached to the arm bones and the long finger bone.

Long finger bone

# FLYING BIRDS

THE wings of flying birds come in many shapes and sizes. Some birds have long wings for gliding, while others have short wings that they flap many times a second.

Buzzard

## HOVERING

This fawn-breasted hummingbird is using its fine flight control to hover in front of a flower and drink its sweet nectar.

{ Fig 1: Flight feathers }

Birds rotate their feathers to different angles during flight to give them maximum lift.

## FLIGHT CONTROL

Hummingbirds are the masters of flight control. They can fly forwards or backwards, or they can hover in the same place. They flap their small wings between 20 and 100 times every second!

Tail feathers help the bird to steer.

## HOLLOW BONES

A flying bird's bones are hollow. They are strong, but light enough for the bird to fly.

The buzzard's large, broad wings make it a strong flier.

Breast muscles

## BREAST POWER

The largest muscles in a bird's body are its breast muscles. The muscles provide the power for the downstroke of the wings. This produces a force, called lift, that keeps the bird in the air.

### Cool beaks

This toucan's beak is nearly half the length of its body. The huge beak has a large surface area, which keeps the bird cool. It is filled with a very light spongy substance.

{ Fig 2: Clark's grebes }

## STAYING TOGETHER

Many birds stay with the same mate for their whole lives. They keep their partnerships strong using special greetings and dances. To seal their partnership, grebes run across the water together with their long necks extended upwards.

# CAPE PENGUIN

PENGUINS use their short wings like flippers and spend most of their lives in the water, where they feed on fish and krill. Penguins live only in the Southern Hemisphere. The Cape penguin lives around the coast of southern Africa.

### HEAVY BONES
Unlike the bones of flying birds, a penguin's bones are heavy. The extra weight helps them to dive more easily.

Wings have flattened bones.

Ribs

Breastbone

Feet are used like a rudder for steering.

Cape penguins swim at an average speed of 7 km/h, but can reach a top speed of 20 km/h when hunting.

# DEEP DIVER

The Cape penguin hunts small fish such as anchovies. It can hold its breath for five minutes at a time and dive to a depth of up to 100 metres. It may swim more than 100 kilometres on a single feeding trip.

Long beak

Cape penguins stand 60 cm tall. The largest species, the emperor penguin, is twice as tall.

Wish bone

Finger bones

## Nesting

Penguins come on land to lay their eggs and raise their young. Cape penguins make their nests on rocky beaches. The female lays two eggs, then both the mother and father take turns looking after them.

## SLEEK SHAPE

Penguins have streamlined bodies. This means that their shape allows them to cut a path through the water as they swim.

# FLIGHTLESS BIRDS

PENGUINS use their wings to swim. Other flightless birds, such as ostriches, have useless wings but can run at high speeds.

## BIG BIRD

The ostrich is the largest bird in the world. It also lays the largest eggs, which weigh more than 1 kilogram. Like other big flightless birds such as the emu, the ostrich is a fast runner, reaching speeds of up to 70 km/h.

### Ground feeder

The kiwi lives in the forests of New Zealand. Its tiny wings are hidden under hair-like feathers. It has a sensitive beak, which it uses to search the forest floor for insects and worms.

Short wings are much too small to use for flying.

Muscular legs

## TOBOGGANING

For these emperor penguins, sliding along the ice is sometimes much easier than walking.

# SENSING DANGER

For many large predators, such as leopards and lions, an ostrich makes a tasty meal. But they are not so easy to catch. Their heads are nearly 3 metres above the ground, which means that they can spot danger from a long way away.

Large eyes give the bird excellent vision.

Long neck

## PORPOISING

Penguins sometimes fly out of the water as they swim in a movement called porpoising. They may do this to confuse predators.

## DEAD AS A DODO

The dodo was a flightless bird that lived on the island of Mauritius in the Indian Ocean. It died out soon after humans arrived on the island. Their eggs were eaten by the dogs and cats that people brought with them.

{ Fig 1: Dodo }

# PLATYPUS

NO other animal on Earth looks quite like the platypus, with its flat duck-like snout. It spends most of its day in the water foraging for food. It feeds on shrimps, insect larvae and worms, which it digs out of the river bed with its sensitive snout.

Legs stick out of the side of the body like a lizard's legs.

## TOOTHLESS
Instead of teeth, adult platypuses have horny pads inside their mouths.

Eye socket

The snout is made of skin stretched over a framework of bone.

## EYES SHUT
The platypus hunts in muddy water where eyes are of little use. In fact, it keeps its eyes tightly shut when it dives. It finds its prey by sensing the electricity that runs through their bodies. It does this with special sense receptors in its snout.

# PADDLING

Platypuses swim by paddling their front legs. They use their back legs and tail to steer.

The platypus is 60 cm long from its head to the end of its tail.

The platypus stores fat in its tail.

Flattened ribcage

Poisonous spur

## Hungry hunter

The platypus has a big appetite and hunts for about ten hours a day. It spends most of the rest of its time asleep in a burrow in the riverbank.

Webbed feet

# MONOTREMES

FOUND in Australia and New Guinea, echidnas and platypuses are monotremes. They are the only mammals that lay eggs.

{ Fig 1: Protective spines }

Long snout acts as both mouth and nose.

## ECHIDNA

The echidna uses its snout to root out ants and termites. Like the platypus, its snout can sense electricity in the bodies of its prey. It grabs the insects with its long, sticky tongue.

## DEFENCE MECHANISM

When threatened, the echidna curls up into a tight ball.

# LAYING EGGS

{ Fig 2: Platypus eggs }

The female platypus lays her eggs in a burrow. The young stay in the burrow for 3-4 months after they hatch, feeding on their mother's milk. When they are big enough, they emerge from the burrow for their first swim.

{ Fig 3: Platypus young }

## SPINES

The head, back and tail of the echidna are covered in sharp spines, which protect it from predators. Baby echidnas, called puggles, are born without spines. The spines start to appear when the puggles are about 50 days old.

### Venomous ankles

Male platypuses have venomous spurs on their rear ankles. They use these weapons in fights with other males.

## WARM FUR

Platypuses are kept warm by their thick fur. The fur has two layers, which work together to trap air next to the skin. The air keeps the skin warm and dry, even when the platypus is diving.

# RED KANGAROO

THE red kangaroo is a large marsupial that lives in the hot deserts of Australia. It has powerful back legs, which it uses to hop along at high speed.

**BACKBONE**
The backbone is strong but flexible. It needs to bend to allow the animal to hop.

### Desert traveller

Red kangaroos feed on grass and leaves. But there are few plants in the desert, so they must travel many kilometres a day to find enough to eat.

This large bone supports the mother's pouch and helps the animal to leap.

The tail has very strong bones. The kangaroo uses its tail to keep its balance as it hops.

Neural spines

Standing upright, a male red kangaroo is 2 metres tall – taller than an adult human.

Eye socket

## GREAT LEAPS

A red kangaroo can leap up to 9 metres in a single hop, and reach a top speed of more than 60 km/h. It can also jump up to a height of 3 metres.

Short front legs

The shin bone is very long. The powerful leg muscles are attached to it.

### DANGER

Red kangaroos have sharp claws and a powerful kick. No predators dare to take on an adult. However, dingoes and eagles will try to take the young.

# MARSUPIALS

MARSUPIALS are mammals that give birth to tiny young, which grow inside a pouch in their mother's body.

## SAFE PLACE

Kangaroo joeys stick their heads out of the pouch for weeks before they feel it is safe to leave.

{ Fig 1: Eastern quoll }

### NIGHT HUNTER

Quolls spend the daytime tucked away in their dens, safe from predators. They come out to hunt at night, feeding on rabbits, small birds and lizards. Quolls have keen senses, with large ears and sensitive noses to help them find prey in the dark.

## BOXING MATCH

Male kangaroos fight each other in boxing matches. They stand on their hind legs and jab at their opponent. The one that stays upright wins the fight.

Fighting kangaroos punch with their front legs.

## Up a gum tree

The koala spends most of its life in eucalyptus trees, also called gum trees, feeding on the leaves. A baby koala clings to its mother's back as she moves around the tree.

## JOEYS

A marsupial baby is called a joey. When it is born, a joey is the size of a bean, and is blind and furless. It crawls across its mother's fur to the pouch, where it latches onto a teat to feed on the mother's milk. The joey stays in the pouch for up to a year.

Tail helps to support the body weight during a fight.

## FIERCE DEVIL

The Tasmanian devil is a bad-tempered hunter. When it is excited, it makes a deafening screech.

43

# FRUIT BAT

FRUIT BATS are the largest bats in the world. Their distinctive heads hold super senses, which they use to track down their food of fruit, nectar or pollen while swooping through the sky. When they find food, they fly up to the branches and grab on using sharp claws.

### "THUMB"

The "thumb" of many bats sticks above the wing to form a claw, which they use to grasp and move about.

Forearm bones

"Finger" Bones

The "fingers" of a bat are very long. Thin flaps of skin stretch between them to form the wings.

## NIGHT VISION

Also known as the "flying fox", this type of bat is easy to spot because of its long, dog-like snout. Inside this is a highly sensitive nose, which the bat uses to sniff out delicious fruit to chew or nectar-rich flowers to lick. Unlike other bats, flying foxes do not use echolocation to find their food and must rely on their heightened sense of smell.

The largest fruit bats have a wingspan that stretches for about 1.7 m, but a body length that's just 40 cm.

A fruit bat's wings can stretch as tall as an adult human.

Skull

Claw

Shoulder

The heaviest flying foxes weigh up to 2 kg, about the weight of two bags of sugar.

Foot

## Tropical resident

Flying foxes are found in the warmer tropical parts of the world where fruit trees and flowers are common. They are even found on some remote islands in the Pacific Ocean.

# BATS

BATS are the only mammals capable of true flight, using their wings to flap through the air.

While some bats use a keen sense of hearing, others have large eyes and rely on their sight.

*[ Fig 1: External ear ]*

## FLYING HUNTER

While flying foxes like to eat fruit and flowers, many bats actively hunt for prey. They are so well suited to hunting in the dark that they can catch insects in mid-air and feed without having to land. Other bats feed in a more sinister way. Vampire bats land on large mammals, bite through the skin and drink the blood!

## THE WINGS

A bat's wings are so thin that the blood vessels running through them are clearly visible.

The long fingers stretch out to form the wings.

Bats that use echolocation have large ears to collect the echoes.

Grey long-eared bat

## SHARP TEETH

Some bats have very sharp teeth to eat insect prey, which they catch in mid-air.

## PIPISTRELLE

These are some of the smallest bats, with a body length of just 4 cm.

### Hearing things

Many bats have a very keen sense of hearing and use sound to detect prey and what is around them. This is called echolocation. They produce a series of high-pitched clicks (so high that humans can't hear them) and listen for echoes made as these clicks bounce off objects or nearby prey.

## FLYING SQUIRRELS

Another mammal that takes to the air is the flying squirrel. It has flaps of skin that stretch between its legs, and it holds these out as wings. However, it is not capable of true flight and uses these wings to glide from tree to tree in its forest home.

{ Fig 2: Before take-off }

{ Fig 3: In flight }

# BEAVER

THE American beaver is a rodent that spends most of its time in the water. Beavers are very hard workers. They cut down trees and use the branches to build their homes.

## FELLING TREES

Beavers can fell trees with trunks up to 1 metre in diameter. They gnaw away at the trunk with their chisel-like front teeth.

### Dam builder

Beavers build dams across shallow streams using a mixture of branches and mud. The dam creates a still pond behind it.

**BIG LUNGS**

A beaver can stay underwater for up to 15 minutes at a time.

Knee

**DANGER SIGNAL**

When they sense danger, beavers signal to each other by slapping the water with their flat tails.

Webbed back feet

A beaver's body is about 70 cm long. It weighs up to 27 kg.

Eyes and nose are at the top of the head.

**FRONT TEETH**
The four large front teeth have razor-sharp edges.

Sharp claws

## SAFE HOUSE

A beaver's home, called a lodge, is a safe shelter for beaver families to sleep. Built in the pond behind their dam, the lodge has underwater entrances safe from predators.

# RODENTS

RODENTS are mammals with a pair of strong front teeth that they use to chew through tough food.

Ears

Eye

Eyes, nose and ears are at the top of the head, which makes swimming easier.

Young capybara sticks close to its mother.

### TREE CLIMBER
The Indian palm squirrel is an expert climber. It feeds on the nuts and fruit of the trees it climbs.

## CAPYBARA
Weighing as much as 50 kilograms, the capybara is the largest rodent in the world. It lives in big family groups in swamps in South America, feeding mostly on grasses.

# NAKED RAT

{ Fig 1: Naked mole rat }

Naked mole rats spend their whole lives underground. They dig tunnels with their front teeth and feed on the roots of plants. The rats live in large colonies of up to 200 animals, which all share the same network of tunnels.

## DESERT RAT

The kangaroo rat lives in deserts. It takes shelter in a burrow during the day. At night, it comes out to feed on seeds, which it stores in special pouches in its cheeks.

Heartbeat slows to save energy as the dormouse sleeps.

## Sleepy mouse

Dormice survive the winter by hibernating. They may sleep for more than six months in a cold year, waking up occasionally to eat from a store of food that they have stashed nearby.

## BIG TEETH

The teeth at the front of rodents' jaws keep growing throughout their lives. This means that the teeth never wear out. The animals gnaw at wood or other hard surfaces to stop the teeth from growing too long.

# LION

THE mighty lion is a big cat. It lives in family groups called prides. Lions hunt large prey such as zebra and wildebeest. They mostly hunt under cover of darkness and rest during the day.

The backbone is very flexible, which allows the lion to crouch as it hunts.

Ribcage

Knee

**TAIL**
The lion swings its tail from side to side as it runs. This helps it to keep its balance.

**MOTHER AND CUBS**
Female lions, called lionesses, care for their cubs and teach them how to hunt.

**CLAWS**
The claws fold backwards when they are not needed. This keeps them sharp.

A fully grown lion is about 2 m long and weighs as much as three adult humans.

# TEETH AND CLAWS

A lion's main weapons are its sharp claws and dagger-like canine teeth. It kills prey by sinking its teeth into its victim's neck.

Large muscles give the jaw a powerful bite.

Canine teeth

## Pride leaders

Most prides are ruled by large, adult males. They have to fight rival males to keep control of their pride.

# SCARY MANES

Male lions are slightly larger than the females. The males have a thick mane of hair around their necks, which makes them look even bigger and more scary.

# CATS

WHETHER they are big or small, cats all look very similar. They are hunters that catch their prey using sharp teeth and claws.

## HIDDEN DANGER

A tiger's stripes break up its shape, making it harder for prey to see it coming.

← Tail

## ROAR OR PURR?

Big cats such as lions and tigers make a blood-chilling roar. The small cats we keep as pets cannot roar, and mew or growl instead. But they can purr continuously, which big cats cannot do.

Hind legs ↗

{ Fig 1: Striped fur }

## BUILT FOR SPEED

The cheetah can run faster than any other land animal, reaching speeds of over 100 km/h. But it can only sprint over short distances, and its prey often escapes.

Cheetahs often live alone, but here two brothers have teamed up to hunt.

A Siberian tiger can cover 10 m in a single leap.

## SMALL CAT

The caracal is a little larger than a domestic cat. Its large ears give it excellent hearing. There are long tufts on the ends of its ears, which it twitches to communicate with other caracals.

*{ Fig 2: Caracal }*

## MOUNTAIN TIGER

The biggest big cat of all is the Siberian tiger, which can grow to over 3 metres long . It lives in the icy mountains of eastern Russia, where it hunts deer and wild boar.

## BLACK JAGUAR

Jaguars live in the forests of South and Central America. Most are orange with black spots, but some have bodies that are almost completely black.

### Danger from above

The leopard spends a lot of its time in trees. When it makes a kill, it drags the body up a tree to store it safely to eat at its leisure. Its spots hide it among the leaves, and it will sometimes leap on unsuspecting prey from above.

# ELEPHANT SEAL

**THE** southern elephant seal is the largest of all seals. It lives in the icy waters of the Southern Ocean. A thick layer of fatty blubber under its skin protects it from the extreme cold.

## DEEP SEA DIVER

Elephant seals dive up to 300 metres down in search of fish. At these depths, water presses hard on their bodies. Bendy cartilage in their ribs stops their chests from breaking under the pressure.

**TOE BONES**
The back feet have long toe bones, which the seal uses to push forwards as it swims.

Tibia and fibula

The leg bones are very short and contained mostly in the seal's body.

## Bull seal

Male seals, called bulls, are twice the size of the females. They fight each other in bloody battles for the right to mate.

Females, called cows, give birth to a single pup.

Heavy skull

Sharp canine teeth

## SWIMMER

Seals are clumsy on land, but they are very skilled swimmers. Their strong, flexible backs allow them to move easily through the water.

The bottom parts of the ribs are made from cartilage.

On land, the seal props itself up on its front flippers.

A male elephant seal is about 5 m long and can weigh more than 3,000 kg.

# SEALS

WITH bodies shaped like torpedos and flippers for feet, these mammals are well suited to life in the water. They are found all over the world, but most prefer the cold waters far from the equator.

{ Fig I: External ear }

Sea lions have visible external ear parts.

## SEA LION

Unlike earless seals, which walk using only their front legs, sea lions can walk on all four legs. Their bodies are covered in thick, short fur.

Short fur

### HIDDEN ON THE ICE

Harp seal pups are born with white fur. This hides them from predators when their mothers leave them alone on the ice.

# EARLESS SEALS

So-called earless seals, such as the elephant seal and the common seal, can still hear. But their ears do not have external flaps. This makes their bodies even more streamlined, allowing them to swim at greater speeds.

## Beach colony

Once a year, these Cape fur seals gather together on a beach to breed. The females give birth, then a few days later they mate with the males.

{ Fig 2: Walrus }

## ❧ WALRUS ❧

The walrus is a large animal that lives in the Arctic Ocean. It has two ivory tusks, which can be up to 1 metre long. The walrus digs out holes in the sea ice with its tusks. This allows it to swim under the ice and still have somewhere to breathe. Sensitive whiskers around its mouth help it to find clams, crabs and other food in the murky water on the ocean floor.

## UNDER THE ICE

The Weddell seal spends most of its life under the sea ice of Antarctica.

## OCEAN HUNTER

The leopard seal is a fearsome hunter. It preys on smaller seals, penguins and fish.

# BLUE WHALE

THE blue whale is the largest animal that has ever lived on Earth. Its heart alone is the size of a small car. This enormous animal feeds on tiny krill just a few centimetres long, but it can eat several million of them in a single meal.

## LIGHTWEIGHT

As it is supported by the water, a whale's skeleton is quite lightweight for its size.

## HIP BONES

The tiny hip bones are not attached to the rest of the skeleton.

Backbone

## DEEP BREATH

A blue whale's lungs can hold 5,000 litres of air at a time. This allows the whale to hold its breath for more than 30 minutes when it dives.

## TAIL BONES

A whale pushes itself through the water by swishing its tail up and down. Large muscles are attached to the spines on the tail bones.

The tail comes above the water as the whale starts a dive.

Shoulder blade

The neck is short to keep the body streamlined.

An adult blue whale is about 30 m long and weighs 170 tonnes.

The jaw bones are long and curved.

The front flippers are each made up of five "fingers".

## ARCTIC FEEDER

The blue whale spends much of the year in the Arctic or Antarctic oceans, where there are plenty of krill to eat. It moves to warmer waters to give birth.

### Protected

Before humans started to hunt them, there were hundreds of thousands of blue whales. Today only about 10,000 are left. But they are now protected by law, and are no longer hunted.

# WHALES AND DOLPHINS

WHALES and dolphins are mammals that spend their whole lives in the water. Some have teeth, while others have baleen plates.

{ Fig 1: Baleen }

The baleen are thick, hairy plates in the grey whale's mouth.

## WHALE SONG
The humpback whale sings songs that can be heard by other whales hundreds of kilometres away.

Eye »

{ Fig 2: Blowholes }

A whale's nostrils, called blowholes, are at the top of its head.

*{ Fig 3: Killer whale }*

## CLEVER WHALE

Killer whales have worked out many different ways to catch prey. Some hunt fish, while others prefer seals or dolphins. This killer whale has beached itself to catch a seal. After catching the seal, it must wriggle its way back into the water before it gets stuck.

## FILTER FEEDERS

Baleen whales, such as the blue whale and the grey whale, feed by filtering creatures from the water. They fill their mouths with water, then squeeze it out through their baleen plates. Any fish or krill in the water are caught in the baleen.

### ACROBATIC DOLPHINS

Common dolphins are a little bigger than humans. They can swim up to 60 km/h and leap high out of the water.

← Jaw

## OCEAN TRAVELLER

Each year, grey whales swim from the Arctic Ocean to the coast of Mexico and back to the Arctic – a round trip of 20,000 kilometres.

### Deep sea hunter

The sperm whale dives to depths of up to 3 kilometres in search of its favourite meal – giant squid. Many of the whales have scars on their bodies from battles with squid.

# AFRICAN ELEPHANT

**ELEPHANTS** are the biggest land animals in the world. The African elephant lives in forests and grasslands. It feeds on leaves, twigs, bark, fruit and roots.

## BACKBONE

The backbone is thick and stiff. Elephants cannot bend over, but must kneel down or reach with their trunks.

Hip bone

## BIG APPETITE

An adult elephant needs to eat 200 kilograms of food every day. That's the same weight as 1,000 apples!

## TALKING FEET

Elephants sense vibrations in the ground with their feet, allowing them to "talk" over great distances. The rumble of their "voices" travels down their legs and through the ground.

A male African elephant may be over 3 m tall and weigh more than 5 tonnes.

The skull is thick and strong to support the weight of the tusks and trunk.

Back teeth are 30 cm across.

Tusks are long front teeth. They may be up to 2 m long.

Leg bones are very thick to support the heavy body.

Each foot has five toes.

## Sensitive trunk

An elephant's trunk is made from its nose and upper lip. The trunk is strong but very sensitive. It can rip branches from a tree or gently stroke a newborn baby.

# ELEPHANTS

FOUND in Africa and Asia, elephants are among the most intelligent animals in the world. They roam the forests and grasslands in close-knit family groups.

## HEAD OF THE FAMILY

Each family group is led by an old female, known as the matriarch. Her experience is vital as she knows where the best places to eat and drink are to be found.

### PLAYING

Elephants enjoy each other's company. Youngsters are often at play, especially when they're in the water.

## WOOLLY MAMMOTH

The woolly mammoth was a large elephant-like creature that lived on the cold northern plains during the last ice age. It died out about 10,000 years ago when the climate warmed up.

{ Fig 1: Woolly mammoth }

{ Fig 2: Mammoth skull }

## Asian elephants

Asian elephants are slightly smaller than their African cousins and have much smaller ears. Only males have long tusks.

# LEAVING HOME

Female elephants stay with their family group for their whole lives. Males leave the group when they grow up to live alone or with other males.

{ Fig 4: Tusk }

Elephants use their tusks to knock down trees and to dig.

The trunk is controlled by 60,000 muscles.

## BIG BABY

A newborn baby elephant weighs more than an adult human.

Large ears help the elephant to lose heat and keep cool.

The nostrils at the end of the trunk have an excellent sense of smell.

{ Fig 3: Nostrils }

# MOOSE

ALSO called the elk, the moose is the largest member of the deer family. It lives in northern forests, where it feeds on shoots and bark.

## BONY ANTLERS

Only male moose have antlers. The antlers start to grow in spring and are full-size by the mating season in autumn. They then drop off in winter.

## DON'T MESS

Moose are big and powerful and scare off most predators. An adult moose can kill a bear or wolf that tries to attack it.

Short tail bone

### Test of strength

Male moose fight each other in tests of strength, called rutting. They push at each other's antlers until the weaker animal gives way.

Knee

## MIDDLE TOES

The moose walks on hoofs formed by its two large middle toes.

Outside toe

## NEURAL SPINES

The neural spines are spikes that stick up from the backbone. Powerful muscles stretch from the neural spines to the back of the skull. The muscles support the weight of the heavy head.

Antlers grow out of the top of the skull. They grow very quickly - more than 1 cm a day.

Shoulder bone

## CALF

The female gives birth in spring. Her calf will stay with her until the following spring, when she chases it away.

Radius

A male moose stands 2 m high at the shoulder and weighs 700 kg - as much as 10 adult humans.

# DEER AND ANTELOPE

DEER and antelope are mammals that walk on the ends of their middle toes. Deer mostly live in cool areas. Most antelope are found on the hot African grasslands.

Long ears

As it feeds, a gerenuk's big ears listen out for the rustling of any predators in the bushes.

{ Fig 1: Gerenuk head }

Long neck

**GERENUK**
This long-necked antelope lives in East Africa.

## ON THE MOVE
Reindeer travel up to 5,000 km each year in search of new pastures. They are strong swimmers and cross wide rivers and lakes on their journeys.

Flexible hip joints allow the gerenuk to stand upright and reach high branches.

## FANGED DEER

Male tufted deer have large tusk-like incisor teeth. They use these fangs to fight off rivals.

### Surviving winter

During the long, cold winter, red deer survive by digging through the snow to eat the grass underneath. They also eat tree bark when snow covers the ground.

# WATCHING OUT

To a lion, a leopard or a hyena, an antelope is a prized catch, so the antelopes must keep a constant look out for predators. Their eyes are positioned on the sides of their heads, which allows them to see to the side as well as to the front.

## INSECT PICKER

The oxpecker is a welcome friend to this impala. The bird picks itchy insects from the impala's fur.

{ Fig 2: Springbok pronking }

## ∞ PRONKING ∞

When they sense danger, springboks leap into the air - an action called pronking. They jump as high as they can, reaching up to 4 m off the ground. The high leaps show potential predators that the springboks are fit and strong, and that the predators had better look elsewhere for their next meal.

# HORSE

## DOMESTICATION

Humans first tamed, or domesticated, wild horses about 6,000 years ago.

**HORSES** are large grass-eating mammals. Most horses are domestic animals, which means that they live with humans. We use horses for transport, to pull farm machinery and for sport.

Neural spines

### TAIL
The horse swishes its tail using muscles attached to spines at the top of the tail.

Knee socket

Hock

Fetlock

### WILD HORSE
The only truly wild horse left in the world is the Przewalski's horse, which lives in Central Asia.

Measured to the tops of their shoulders, horses are between 1.4 and 1.8 m tall.

First thoracic vertebra

Eye socket

Nose bone

Long jaws contain rows of molar teeth for chewing grass.

Wide ribcage protects large lungs.

## Herd animals

Horses live together in herds. Each herd has a herd leader who decides what the herd should do.

# LIGHT FEET

Horses have just one long toe on each foot. At the tip of each toe is a bone called the coffin bone, which is protected by the horny hoof. A horse's feet are narrow and light, which allows it to pick its legs up very quickly and gallop at high speed.

At the end of each toe is a tough hoof.

# HORSES, ZEBRAS AND DONKEYS

ZEBRAS are wild animals that live on the plains and mountains of Africa. Horses and donkeys are mostly domestic animals that live and work with humans.

## BORN TO RUN

Horses and zebras run using a movement called a gallop. Racehorses can keep up a gallop of over 60 km/h for more than a kilometre.

Galloping horses

### Kicking out

When they are cornered, zebras and horses have a powerful weapon. They rear up on their front legs and kick out at an attacker with their hind legs.

## MOOR PONIES

Ponies are small horses. These Dartmoor ponies need to be very hardy to survive on the wet and windy moorland.

## BEAST OF BURDEN

A mule is the offspring of a male donkey and a female horse. It is faster than a donkey but can work longer hours than a horse. Mules are used in mountainous parts of the world to carry cargo across rough terrain.

{ Fig 1: Mules }

## BRAYING DONKEYS

Donkeys make a loud braying noise. Their big ears can hear the brays of other donkeys up to 3 km away.

Horses' hooves are often fitted with metal shoes to give them extra protection.

{ Fig 2: Hoof }

# THREE-TOED SLOTH

At the end of each toe is a hook-shaped claw about 8 cm long.

YOU could easily walk right under a sloth without seeing it. A sloth spends most of its time motionless, hanging upside down from a tree and blending in with the leafy canopy.

Three-toed feet

## SWIMMING

Sloths are good swimmers. Sometimes they drop straight into a river from the trees to swim to a new location.

## NIGHT FEEDER

Sloths eat and sleep in the trees. They rest during the day and feed at night. They come down to the ground about once a week to poo.

## Green camouflage

A sloth's brown fur has a green tinge to it. This is caused by algae growing in the fur. The green colour helps to hide the animal from predators such as eagles.

**LONG ARMS**
The sloth pulls itself from branch to branch using its long front legs.

Shoulder bone

**LONG NECK**
There are nine bones in a sloth's neck. It is long and flexible, which allows the sloth to look down at the ground while it hangs.

Teeth are worn down by years of chewing tough leaves.

A three-toed sloth is about 50 cm long and weighs 4–5 kg – the size of a large domestic cat.

# TREE MAMMALS

THE dense rainforests of South America are home to many different mammals. Monkeys swing acrobatically through the canopy. Sloths, on the other hand, keep as still as they can.

## USEFUL TAIL
Amazonian monkeys use their tails to grip onto branches.

## HOWLERS
Howler monkeys call to each other from the treetops. Their piercing howls can be clearly heard up to 5 km away.

The tail has a hairless tip that is grooved to give a good grip.

## FOREST MONKEYS
More than 100 different species of monkey make their home in the Amazon rainforest. They have long tails that they use as an extra limb to swing from branch to branch.

Black-handed spider monkey

# BELLY CRAWL

The sloth's long arms and hooked claws are perfect for hanging from branches, but very bad for walking. When it comes down to the ground, it has to drag itself along with its claws. It returns to the safety of the trees as soon as it can.

{ Fig 1: Three-toed sloth }

## Hang on tight

Baby sloths cling to their mothers for the first nine months of their lives. When the baby grows up, its mother leaves it alone and finds herself a new territory.

## TWO-TOED SLOTH

The two-toed sloth is slightly larger and more energetic than its three-toed relative.

Strong hands

## SLOW DIGESTION

Sloths feed mostly on thick leaves. A sloth needs long periods of sleep and rest in between feeding so that it can digest its tough diet.

## SLOTH FEEDING

A sloth holds a branch still with its claws as it munches on the leaves.

# GIANT ANTEATER

There is a small hump at the back of the neck. The neck is thicker than the head.

THIS large mammal lives on a diet of ants and termites. It tears open an ants' nest with its claws, then flicks out its tongue. The tongue is covered in tiny spines, which catch the ants.

## HYOID BONES

The tongue is moved by the hyoid bones. Muscles attached to the hyoid can flick the tongue in and out of the mouth up to three times a second.

Long snout

Broad ribs

The anteater walks on its front knuckles, with its long claws curled up.

## BUSHY TAIL

The anteater's body is covered in long hairs. When it sleeps, it uses its bushy tail like a blanket, covering its body to keep warm.

From nose to tail, a giant anteater is about 2 m long. Its head is about 30 cm long.

Special joints give the backbone extra strength.

# NEST RAIDER

A giant anteater will dig up about 200 nests in a day. The ants and termites fight back with stinging bites, and the anteater is forced out after about a minute. This means that enough insects will survive for the colony to recover.

← Tail

← Thigh bone

## Hidden pup

Female anteaters carry their pups on their backs. The markings on the pup's fur line up with its mother's markings. This hides the pup from predators.

## TOOTHLESS

With tube-like jaws and no teeth, an anteater does not chew its food. It crushes insects against its palate before swallowing them whole.

# ANTEATERS

Large ears give a sharp sense of hearing.

FOUND only in the Americas, slow-moving anteaters are closely related to sloths. They are shy animals, but will attack if backed into a corner.

## DEFENCE POSE

When it feels threatened, the tamandua (a type of anteater) rears up on its hind legs to attack with its front claws. It also gives off a foul-smelling gas from glands in its anus.

Southern tamandua

## DIGGER

The tamandua's forearms have strong muscles. It needs them to dig open ant and termite nests.

Long tail

{ Fig 1: Tongue }

A giant anteater's tongue is more than 50 cm long – longer than its head.

## SNIFFING AROUND

Anteaters have small eyes and poor eyesight. But their noses are around 40 times more sensitive than a human nose. They sniff their way to their meals.

## CLAWS

The claws on the two middle fingers are long, curved digging tools. They also make  fearsome weapons.

## Silky anteater

The silky anteater gets its name from the silk cotton trees in which it lives. It holds on to the tree's branch with its back legs and tail while it searches for insects with its front arms.

## ARMADILLOS

With tough, leathery armour covering their backs and heads, armadillos are well protected against predators. They dig out deep burrows to sleep in during the day, coming out at night to hunt for insects.

{ Fig 2: Pink fairy armadillo }

{ Fig 3: Nine-banded armadillo }

# GORILLA

GORILLAS are apes that live in the dense forests of central Africa. They are large and powerful, but spend most of their time feeding peacefully on plants.

## MOUNTAIN GORILLAS

Some gorilla groups live high in the mountains. They have thicker fur to keep them warm in the cold conditions.

## FAMILY GROUP

Gorillas live in small groups of about 10, with one large male and several females and their young. The male defends the group from attackers.

## KNUCKLE WALKING

A gorilla usually walks on all fours, leaning on its knuckles. Its arms are longer than its legs, making walking on all fours easier.

Thigh bone

Legs are very straight, making walking upright difficult.

The big toe can touch all the other toes, allowing the gorilla to hold objects with its feet.

Bony ridge on the forehead protects the eyes.

## TEETH

Adult gorillas have 32 teeth - the same number as all other apes, including humans.

A male gorilla stands about 1.8 m tall. This is the same height as a human, but a gorilla is much heavier - up to four times the weight.

## Silverback

At about the age of 12, male gorillas grow white hairs on their backs. When they are fully grown, the males will leave their group to start their own families.

Gorillas walk on their front knuckles.

# APES

THE apes are a group of primates that includes human beings. They have expressive faces, which they use to show each other how they are feeling.

Chimps and bonobos are our closest relatives of all the apes.

Bonobo infant

Bonobo mother

## USING TOOLS

This chimpanzee is crushing nuts using a piece of wood as a tool.

Female bonobos form close bonds with their sons, which will last for their whole lives.

## SOCIAL GROUPS

Chimpanzees and bonobos look very similar, but live in different kinds of social group. Chimp groups are dominated by males, and order is kept by the threat of violence. In bonobo groups, the females dominate and there is less violent conflict.

# SWINGING GIBBON

Gibbons are extraordinary acrobats. swinging through the trees at speeds of up to 56 km/h. They can cover 15 metres in a single leap. They also walk along branches on two legs, their long arms stretched out for balance like a tightrope-walker's pole.

## GREAT APES

Unlike monkeys, apes have no visible tails. There are two groups of apes. The great apes include chimps, gorillas, orangutans and humans. The lesser apes, or gibbons, are smaller and more agile than the great apes.

### Man of the forest

Orangutans, whose name means "man of the forest", live in the rainforests of Borneo and Sumatra. They spend most of their time in the trees.

### CHEST BEATER

When they are threatened, gorillas beat their chests with their fists and make a loud hooting sound to intimidate their opponents.

The rounded skull protects our large brains. The skull is made of 22 bones: 21 bones tightly fused together to make a hard case, plus a hinged jawbone.

## RIBCAGE

The ribcage is a framework of bones that protects our lungs and heart. As we breathe in, muscles pull at the ribcage to make it larger to make room for the lungs to fill with air.

Elbow

Bowl-shaped hip bones.

# HUMAN

WE are the only apes that walk all the time on two legs. This frees up our hands to explore the world. To help us make full use of our hands, we have developed very big brains that allow us to think and solve problems.

## ALL-ROUND ATHLETES

Humans can run, jump, swim, climb and throw. Our all-round skills allow us to survive in many different kinds of habitat.

There are 27 bones in each hand.

# FLEXIBLE THUMBS

Our thumbs have flexible joints that allow them to touch any of the fingers. This allows us to pick up objects and turn them around in our hands to examine them.

Flat feet with short toes provide a solid platform for walking.

Long thigh bone

Knee cap

There are 26 bones in each foot.

The thigh bones are angled to place the legs right under our bodies. This makes walking on two legs much easier.

## Baby bones

A newborn baby's skeleton is made of more than 300 bones. As the baby grows, some of these bones join together, and an adult human skeleton has just 206 bones.

# AMAZING BONE FACTS

### BIGGEST BONE

The largest bone in the animal kingdom is the jawbone of the blue whale. It is up to 6 metres long and weighs about 600 kilogrammes. That's as heavy as a small car.

### LONG NECK

A giraffe's neck is 2 metres long. It is made up of seven bones. That's the same number of bones as there are in the human neck, but a giraffe's neck bones are much longer.

Each neck bone is nearly 30 cm long.

Blue whale jawbone

Bone marrow

### BLOOD FACTORY

Bones are hard and stiff, but they are also alive. Nerves and blood vessels run through them. At the centre of many bones is a soft substance called bone marrow. One of the bone marrow's jobs is to make red blood cells. The bones in your body make 2 million new blood cells every second!

### TUSKED WHALE

The narwhal has a single tusk that grows up to 3 metres long. The tusk is its left canine tooth. It is hollow and light, weighing about 10 kilogrammes.

## SHARK TEETH

A great white shark has about 300 razor-sharp teeth, arranged in up to seven rows. When a tooth falls out, another grows back in its place.

Tooth has a saw-like edge to rip flesh.

Actual size

Tail

## BREAKING BONES

Lizards can deliberately break off part of their skeleton. They lose their tails to escape from the jaws of a predator. A new tail grows back in a few weeks.

## EAR BONES

The smallest bones in the human body are three tiny bones in the ear called the hammer, the anvil and the stirrup. These bones carry vibrations from the eardrum into the inner ear, where they are heard as sounds.

Actual size

## LONG THIGH

The longest bone in the human body is the thigh bone, or femur. It is almost one third of the length of the whole body.

## FLOATING BONE

The only bone in the human body that is not joined to another bone at a joint is the hyoid bone in the throat.

## FEET AND HANDS

More than half the bones in the human body are found in the feet and hands.

# BONE NAMES

Back vertebrae

THIS lion's bones have been separated to show you all the main parts that make up an animal's skeleton.

Pelvis (hip bone)

Rib

Tail vertebrae

Femur (thigh bone)

Patella (kneecap)

Tibia

Fibula

## SCIENTIFIC NAMES

Many of the bones in a skeleton have two names - their common name and a scientific name. The scientific name usually refers to the bone's shape. For instance, the scientific name for the kneecap is "patella", which is Latin for "little pan".

Tarsals (ankle bones)

Metatarsals (foot bones)

92

Neck vertebrae

Skull

Canine tooth

Carnassial tooth

Mandible (jawbone)

Clavicle (collarbone)

Scapula (shoulder blade)

Humerus

Sternum (breastbone)

Ulna

Radius

## BACKBONE

Every animal in this book has a backbone. A backbone is made from the neck vertebrae, back vertebrae and tail vertebrae.

Phalanges (toe or finger bones)

Claws

Claws

# GLOSSARY

## AMPHIBIAN
An animal that can live on land and in water. Many amphibians start their lives as larvae living in water, then emerge onto land as adults.

## BALEEN
Plates made of keratin inside the mouths of whales such as humpback whales and blue whales. The whales use the baleen plates to filter small fish and krill from the water.

## BEAK
The hard mouthparts of a bird and some other animals, such as turtles. Birds' beaks come in many shapes, depending on their diet. Also called a bill.

## BIRD
An animal with feathers whose front limbs are wings. Birds lay eggs and are warm-blooded, meaning that they keep their temperature constant.

## BLOWHOLE
A hole at the top of the heads of whales and dolphins. The animals only breathe through their blowholes, not through their mouths.

## CARTILAGE
A flexible substance found at the joints of bones, in the rib cage, and in our noses. A shark's whole skeleton is made of cartilage.

## ECHOLOCATION
A system of sounds used by animals such as bats and dolphins to find prey and move around in the dark. Sounds bounce off an object and the animal judges the object's position by listening to the echo.

## FINS
Flaps on the sides of sea creatures such as fish and whales that they use to swim.

## FISH
Animals that live in water and breathe using gills. Fish use muscles attached to their backbones and fins to move their bodies in an "S" shape.

## FLIPPERS
Limbs of some sea-going animals that are used for swimming. In penguins, the wings have adapted to become flippers. In turtles and seals, the flippers are their modified arms and legs.

## GILL
A body part in fish and some amphibians that allows them to breathe underwater. The gills take in oxygen that is dissolved in the water.

## GLAND
A body part that makes chemicals to control processes such as growth. Some animals have glands that make poisons or smelly chemicals that they use to attack other animals.

## HIBERNATE
To go into a deep sleep-like state to survive the cold of winter. When animals hibernate, their bodies cool and their heart rate slows down to save energy.

## HOOF
The horny tip of the toes of some mammals, which they use to walk on. Sheep, deer, and pigs have two hooves on each foot. Horses and zebras have just one on each foot.

## ICE AGE
A period when large parts of the planet are covered in snow and ice. There have been many ice ages in Earth's history. The last ice age ended about 10,000 years ago.

## INVERTEBRATE
An animal that does not have a backbone. Most animals are invertebrates. Some, such as insects, have a hard outer exoskeleton. Others, such as worms and squid, have completely soft bodies.

## KERATIN
A tough protein that our hair and nails are made from. The scales, horns, shells and hooves of many animals are also made of keratin.

## KRILL
Small shrimp-like creatures that are found in large numbers in the oceans. They vary in size from 1 to 15 centimetres long. Krill are the main food of many fish, squid and whales.

## LARVAE
The young of animals such as fish, insects and amphibians. The larvae often look completely different from the adults, and can live in very different places. For example, the larvae of frogs, called tadpoles, live under water, while the adults live mostly on land.

## MAMMAL
A group of warm-blooded animals that have hairy bodies. Female mammals produce milk from glands in their skin, which they use to feed their young.

## MARSUPIAL
A group of mammals that give birth to very small young, which the mothers carry in a pouch while they grow. Marsupials include kangaroos, koalas and opossums.

## MUSCLE
A body part that can contract or squeeze. Muscles are attached to bones to move them around.

## PRIMATE
A group of mammals that have large brains. Primates have hands or feet that can grasp and pick up objects. Monkeys, chimpanzees and humans are all primates.

## REPTILE
A group of animals that have scaly skin and lay eggs. Reptiles are cold-blooded, which means they cannot keep their body temperature constant. Crocodiles, turtles and lizards are all reptiles.

## SCALES
Small protective plates that form part of the outer skin of some animals. Fish have bony scales, while reptiles and birds have scales made of keratin.

## SOCIAL GROUP
A collection of animals of the same species, often closely related to each other, who work together to find food or shelter.

## SPECIES
A kind of living thing. Members of the same species are very similar to one another and can breed and produce offspring.

## TUSK
An enlarged tooth that sticks out of an animal's mouth. Elephants and walruses have two tusks in their upper jaws.

## VERTEBRATE
An animal with a backbone. The backbone is a row of bones called vertebrae. Running through the vertebrae is a spinal cord, which is a bundle of nerves that carry messages between the brain and other parts of the body.

# INDEX